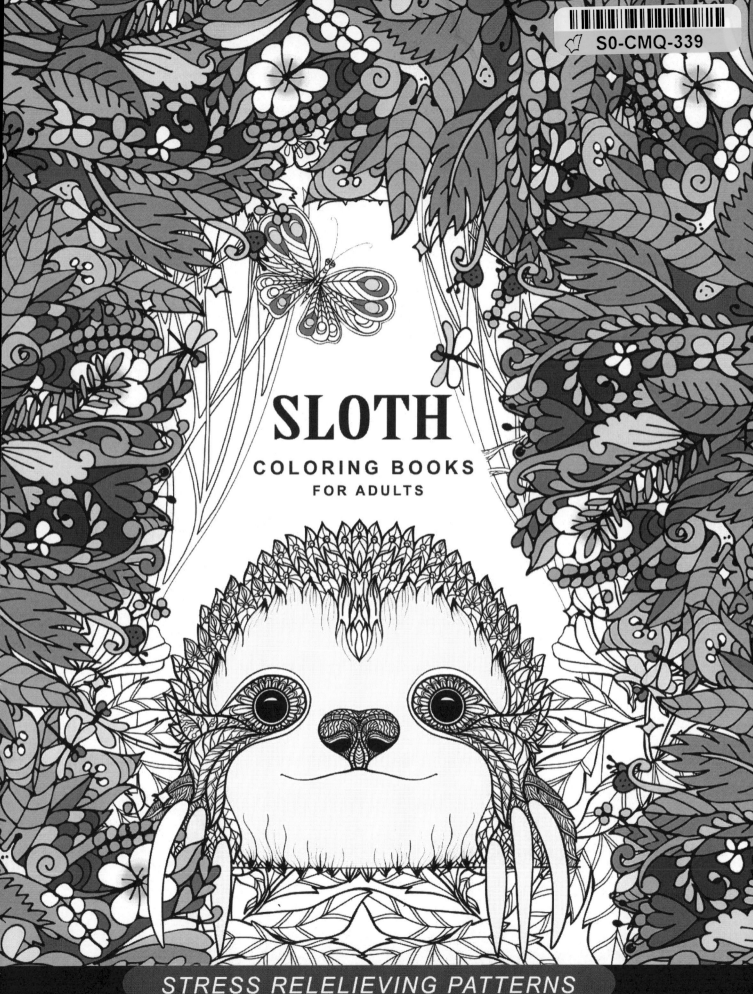

SLOTH

COLORING BOOKS
FOR ADULTS

STRESS RELELIEVING PATTERNS

S0-CMQ-339

SMILE SLOTH

Copyright 2017
Printed in The U.S.A.

All right reserved. This Coloring books or any potion thereof many not be reproduced or used in any manner whatsoever without the exoress written permission of the publisher except.

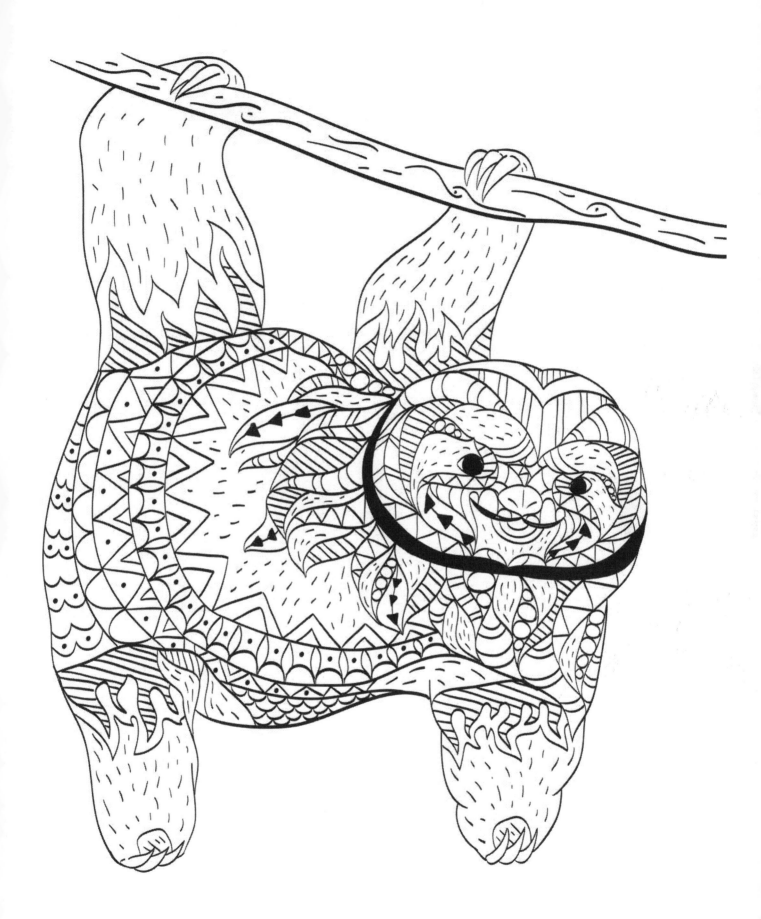

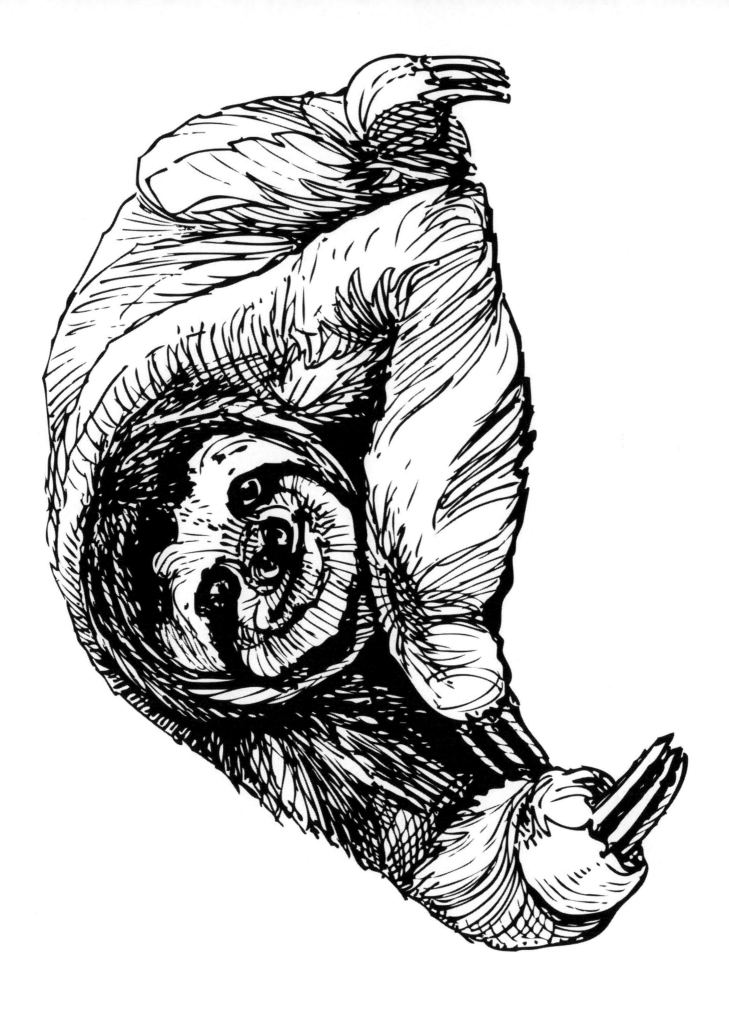

39337867R00033

Made in the USA
Lexington, KY
16 May 2019